# Kush Kingdom Sunrise To Sunset

Teadi Peter

Published by Teadi Peter, 2024.

KUSH KINGDOM SUNRISE TO SUNSET

**First edition. April 30, 2024.**



ISBN: 979-8224168637

Written by Teadi Peter.

# Table of Contents

# The Origins of Kush: Tracing the Roots of an Ancient African Civilization

"From Sunrise to Sunset: The Rise and Fall of the Kush Kingdom" is a captivating exploration of one of ancient Africa's most enigmatic civilizations. Delve into the rich history of the Kush Kingdom, tracing its origins from the dawn of civilization along the Nile River to its eventual decline and disappearance from the historical stage. Uncover the remarkable achievements of the Kushites, from their mastery of architecture and engineering to their influential role in trade and diplomacy. Witness the glory of Kush at its zenith, as it stood as a formidable rival to the mighty empires of Egypt and Rome. Yet, as the sun sets on Kush, follow the kingdom's journey through challenges and conflicts, leading to its eventual demise and the legacy it leaves behind. Through meticulous research and engaging storytelling, this book offers a comprehensive account of the Kush Kingdom's remarkable rise and fall, shedding light on a civilization that continues to fascinate and inspire to this day.

From its humble beginnings as a small kingdom to its rise as a powerful empire, the origins of Kush hold clues to the early development of African civilization and its enduring legacy in the annals of history. In this exploration, we embark on a journey to unravel the origins of Kush, tracing its evolution from a regional power to a force to be reckoned with in the ancient world.

## Exploring the Geographical and Environmental Context of the Kushite Kingdom

The Kingdom of Kush, one of the most significant civilizations of ancient Africa, flourished along the banks of the Nile River in what is now Sudan. The geographical and environmental context of Kush played a crucial role in shaping its development, economy, and culture. In this chapter, we will delve into the geographical features, natural resources, and environmental conditions that influenced the rise and expansion of the Kushite Kingdom.

### The Nile River: Lifeblood of Kush

Central to the geographical context of Kush was the Nile River, which served as the lifeblood of the kingdom. The Nile, the longest river in the world, flows northward through the heart of Africa, bringing water, nutrients, and fertility to the lands along its banks. The annual flooding of the Nile deposited rich silt onto the floodplains, creating fertile soil ideal for agriculture.

The Kushite Kingdom benefited immensely from the fertile lands of the Nile Valley, which allowed for the cultivation of crops such as wheat, barley, sorghum, and flax. The abundance of food provided by agriculture supported the growth of towns and cities, facilitated trade and commerce, and enabled the development of a complex society.

The Nile also served as a vital transportation route, allowing for the movement of people, goods, and ideas between different regions of Kush and beyond. The river provided access to trade networks that extended throughout the Nile Valley and beyond, connecting Kush with neighboring civilizations such as Egypt, Nubia, and the Red Sea coast.

**Natural Resources and Landscapes:**

In addition to the fertile lands of the Nile Valley, the Kushite Kingdom was endowed with a wealth of natural resources and diverse landscapes. To the west of the Nile lay the Western Desert, a vast expanse of arid sand dunes and rocky plateaus that served as a natural barrier against invasion and encroachment from the west.

To the east of the Nile lay the Eastern Desert, a rugged and inhospitable region characterized by rocky mountains, wadis, and desert plains. Despite its harsh conditions, the Eastern Desert was rich in minerals such as gold, copper, and semi-precious stones, which were mined by the Kushites and traded with neighboring civilizations.

To the south of the Nile lay the regions of Upper Nubia and Lower Nubia, which were home to a diverse array of environments, including savannahs, grasslands, and tropical forests. These regions were inhabited by pastoralist communities who herded cattle, sheep, and goats, as well as hunter-gatherer groups who subsisted on wild game, fish, and foraged plants.

**Environmental Challenges and Adaptations:**

While the Nile River provided many benefits to the Kushite Kingdom, it also posed challenges and risks. The annual flooding of the Nile could be unpredictable, causing devastation to crops, settlements, and infrastructure. To mitigate the effects of flooding, the Kushites developed sophisticated irrigation systems, including canals, dikes, and reservoirs, which allowed them to control the flow of water and regulate agricultural production.

The arid and semi-arid regions of Kush also presented challenges to agriculture and settlement. In these areas, the Kushites practiced nomadic pastoralism, moving their herds of livestock between seasonal grazing grounds in search of water and pasture. The harsh conditions of the desert required the Kushites to develop adaptive strategies for survival, including the construction of temporary shelters, the use of drought-resistant crops, and the storage of food and water supplies.

The geographical and environmental context of the Kushite Kingdom played a fundamental role in shaping its development, economy, and culture. The Nile River, with its fertile lands and abundant water supply, provided the foundation for agriculture, settlement, and trade. The diverse landscapes and natural resources of Kush offered opportunities for resource exploitation, economic development, and cultural exchange.

Despite the challenges posed by environmental factors such as flooding, aridity, and fluctuating water levels, the Kushites demonstrated remarkable resilience, adaptability, and ingenuity in overcoming these obstacles. By harnessing the resources of their environment and developing innovative techniques for survival, the Kushites were able to build a thriving civilization that endured for centuries and left a lasting legacy in the annals of ancient African history.

# Nubian Tribes and Early Settlement in Kush: Tracing the Origins of a Civilization

The ancient land of Kush, nestled along the banks of the Nile River in present-day Sudan, was home to a rich tapestry of Nubian tribes whose early settlements laid the foundations for one of the most significant civilizations of ancient Africa. In this exploration, we delve into the origins and early settlement patterns of the Nubian tribes in Kush, tracing their evolution from small farming communities to the emergence of a powerful kingdom.

**Origins of the Nubian Tribes:**

The Nubian tribes of Kush trace their ancestry back to the indigenous peoples of northeastern Africa who inhabited the Nile Valley and surrounding regions for millennia. These early inhabitants were skilled hunters, gatherers, and fishers who relied on the fertile lands of the Nile for their sustenance.

Over time, these small bands of hunter-gatherers began to settle along the banks of the Nile, establishing permanent villages and engaging in subsistence agriculture. The transition from a nomadic to a sedentary way of life marked the beginning of the formation of distinct tribal communities, each with its own social organization, customs, and traditions.

**Early Settlement Patterns:**

The early settlements of the Nubian tribes in Kush were characterized by their proximity to the Nile River and its tributaries, which provided essential resources such as water, fertile soil, and transportation routes. These settlements were often located on elevated terraces or floodplains, which offered protection from seasonal flooding while allowing for easy access to water for irrigation and agriculture.

The layout of these early settlements varied depending on factors such as topography, climate, and social organization. Some villages were small and clustered around a central communal space, while others were larger and more dispersed, with individual households separated by fields and orchards.

**Social Organization and Governance:**

The Nubian tribes of Kush were organized into kinship-based clans or lineages, each headed by a chief or elder who served as a leader and mediator within the community. These chiefs were responsible for maintaining order, resolving disputes, and ensuring the welfare of their members.

In addition to clan leaders, early Nubian settlements in Kush may have also had religious or spiritual leaders who played important roles in ritual ceremonies, healing practices, and community cohesion. These religious leaders, often known as shamans or priests, served as intermediaries between the spiritual and earthly realms, offering guidance, protection, and divine favor to their followers.

**Economic Activities and Subsistence Strategies:**

The economy of early Nubian settlements in Kush was based primarily on agriculture, with the cultivation of crops such as wheat, barley, sorghum, and flax forming the backbone of the local economy. The fertile soils of the Nile Valley, enriched by the annual flooding of the river, provided ideal conditions for agriculture, allowing the Nubian tribes to grow surplus crops for trade and exchange.

In addition to agriculture, the Nubian tribes of Kush engaged in a variety of economic activities, including fishing, hunting, herding, and craft production. Fishermen plied the waters of the Nile and its tributaries, while hunters pursued wild game in the surrounding forests and savannahs. Herders grazed their cattle, sheep, and goats on the grasslands and pastures, while artisans crafted pottery, tools, and ornaments from locally available materials.

**Interactions and Exchange:**

The early Nubian settlements of Kush were not isolated entities but were part of a larger network of interactions and exchange that connected them with neighboring tribes and civilizations. Trade routes crisscrossed the Nile Valley, linking Kush with Egypt to the north, Nubia to the south, and the Red Sea coast to the east.

These trade networks facilitated the exchange of goods, ideas, and technologies between different regions, fostering cultural exchange, economic development, and social integration. The Nubian tribes of Kush traded agricultural products, livestock, and crafts with their neighbors, while also importing luxury goods such as ivory, gold, and exotic spices.

The early settlement of the Nubian tribes in Kush marked the beginning of a long and rich history of civilization in northeastern Africa. From their humble beginnings as small farming communities along the banks of the Nile, the Nubian tribes of Kush would eventually rise to prominence as a powerful kingdom that rivaled the great civilizations of Egypt, Mesopotamia, and Greece.

The origins of the Nubian tribes in Kush are a testament to the ingenuity, resilience, and adaptability of the peoples of ancient Africa, who thrived in the harsh and unforgiving environment of the Nile Valley. By harnessing the resources of their natural surroundings and building vibrant communities based on cooperation and mutual support, the Nubian tribes laid the foundations for the emergence of one of the most significant civilizations of the ancient world.

# The Kushite Contact with Egypt: A Tale of Diplomacy, Conflict, and Cultural Exchange

The relationship between the Kingdom of Kush and its northern neighbor Egypt is a fascinating chapter in the annals of ancient African history. From the earliest interactions between the two civilizations to the conquests of Kushite kings over Egypt, their contact was characterized by a complex interplay of diplomacy, conflict, and cultural exchange. In this chapter, we explore the dynamics of Kushite-Egyptian relations, tracing their evolution from mutual cooperation to outright confrontation.

**Early Interactions and Cultural Exchange:**

The Kingdom of Kush, located to the south of Egypt along the Nile River, had close geographical proximity to its northern neighbor. As early as the Old Kingdom period (c. 2686–2181 BCE), Kushite tribes had established trade and diplomatic ties with Egypt, exchanging goods, ideas, and technologies along the Nile Valley.

One of the most significant aspects of Kushite-Egyptian relations was the exchange of cultural and religious practices. The Kushites adopted many aspects of Egyptian civilization, including the worship of Egyptian gods, the use of hieroglyphic writing, and the construction of monumental architecture inspired by Egyptian designs.

Similarly, the Egyptians were influenced by Kushite culture, adopting Nubian artistic motifs, architectural styles, and religious beliefs. This cultural exchange enriched both civilizations and contributed to the development of a shared cultural heritage that transcended geographical boundaries.

**Diplomatic Relations and Alliance:**

Throughout much of their history, Kush and Egypt maintained diplomatic relations characterized by mutual respect and cooperation.

The Kushite rulers of Napata and Meroe paid tribute to the pharaohs of Egypt and acknowledged their suzerainty, while also asserting their independence and autonomy.

One of the most notable examples of Kushite-Egyptian alliance was during the reign of the Twenty-Fifth Dynasty (c. 760–656 BCE), also known as the Kushite Dynasty. The Kushite kings of this dynasty, such as Piye (Piankhi) and Taharqa, ruled over both Kush and Egypt, establishing their capital at Napata and extending their authority northward into the Nile Delta.

During this period, Kushite-Egyptian relations reached their zenith, with the Kushite pharaohs sponsoring massive building projects, temple constructions, and religious revivals in Egypt. The Kushites also played a crucial role in defending Egypt from foreign invaders, such as the Assyrians and the Persians, who sought to conquer the Nile Valley.

**Conflict and Conquest:**

Despite periods of cooperation and alliance, Kushite-Egyptian relations were not always peaceful, and conflicts occasionally erupted between the two kingdoms. One of the most significant conflicts occurred during the reign of the Twenty-Fifth Dynasty, when the Kushite kings invaded and conquered Egypt, establishing their rule over the land of the pharaohs.

The conquest of Egypt by the Kushites marked a dramatic shift in the balance of power in the region and led to a period of cultural and political integration between the two kingdoms. The Kushite pharaohs adopted many aspects of Egyptian culture and government, while also maintaining their own distinct cultural identity and traditions.

However, Kushite rule over Egypt was relatively short-lived, and by the late 7th century BCE, the Assyrians had expelled the Kushites from Egypt and restored native Egyptian rule. Despite their defeat, the Kushites left behind a lasting legacy in Egypt, with their monuments, inscriptions, and artworks serving as a testament to their influence and impact on Egyptian civilization.

The contact between Kush and Egypt was a dynamic and multifaceted relationship that shaped the history and culture of both civilizations. From the exchange of goods and ideas to the conflicts and conquests that defined their interactions, Kushite-Egyptian relations were characterized by a complex interplay of cooperation, competition, and cultural exchange.

Despite the challenges and conflicts that arose between the two kingdoms, their contact ultimately enriched both civilizations and contributed to the development of a shared cultural heritage that continues to resonate in the modern world. As we continue to study and explore the history of Kushite-Egyptian relations, we gain a deeper appreciation for the complexities of ancient African history and the enduring legacy of its remarkable civilizations.

# Napata: The Dawn of Kushite Civilization

Napata, the first capital of Kush, holds a special place in the annals of ancient African history. Situated along the banks of the Nile River in present-day Sudan, Napata served as the political, religious, and cultural center of the Kushite kingdom for centuries, playing a crucial role in shaping the destiny of the region. In this exploration, we delve into the rich history of Napata, tracing its origins, significance, and enduring legacy in the development of Kushite civilization.

**Origins and Early Settlement:**

The origins of Napata can be traced back to the early Bronze Age, around 3000 BCE, when small farming communities began to settle along the banks of the Nile in northeastern Africa. These early inhabitants practiced agriculture, fishing, and animal husbandry, building simple mud-brick dwellings and pottery vessels to meet their basic needs.

Over time, these small settlements grew into larger communities, as the fertile lands of the Nile Valley attracted more settlers and fostered the development of complex societies. The region's abundant water supply, fertile soil, and temperate climate made it an ideal location for human habitation and agricultural development, laying the foundations for the rise of the Kushite civilization.

**Rise of Napata as the Capital of Kush:**

By the early 8th century BCE, Napata had emerged as a powerful city-state and the capital of the Kingdom of Kush. Under the rule of King Alara, the first ruler of the Twenty-Fifth Dynasty, Napata expanded its territory and influence, establishing diplomatic and commercial ties with neighboring kingdoms and empires, including Egypt to the north and Nubia to the south.

One of the defining features of Napata was its strategic location along the trade routes that connected the civilizations of North Africa, the Middle East, and the Mediterranean. The city served as a hub for the exchange of goods, ideas, and cultures, facilitating the flow of trade and commerce between East and West.

**Cultural and Architectural Achievements:**

During its heyday, Napata was a center of artistic and architectural innovation, with monumental buildings, temples, and palaces dotting its skyline. The city's most iconic landmark was the Temple of Amun, a massive structure dedicated to the worship of the Egyptian god Amun-Ra, which served as the focal point of religious life in Napata.

The architecture of Napata reflected the influence of both Egyptian and Nubian styles, blending elements of both traditions to create a unique and distinctive aesthetic. The city's buildings were constructed using locally available materials such as sandstone, limestone, and mud brick, and adorned with intricate carvings, reliefs, and hieroglyphic inscriptions.

**Napatan Kings and Queens:**

Napata was ruled by a succession of kings and queens who traced their lineage back to the legendary founders of Kushite civilization. One of the most famous rulers of Napata was King Piye, also known as Piankhi, who reigned during the 8th century BCE and is credited with unifying Egypt and Kush under his rule.

Piye's conquest of Egypt marked the beginning of the Twenty-Fifth Dynasty, also known as the Kushite Dynasty, which ruled over both kingdoms for nearly a century. The Kushite kings and queens of Napata left behind a rich legacy of monumental architecture, royal tombs, and inscriptions that shed light on their achievements and aspirations.

**Decline and Legacy:**

Despite its prosperity and power, Napata began to decline in the 4th century BCE, weakened by internal strife, external invasions, and the rise of competing powers in the region. The city was eventually abandoned as the capital of Kush, its former glory fading into obscurity as new centers of power emerged elsewhere in the kingdom.

Today, the ruins of Napata stand as a testament to the ingenuity, resilience, and creativity of the peoples of ancient Africa. The city's monumental architecture, royal tombs, and inscriptions provide valuable insights into the history, culture, and civilization of Kush, preserving the memory of its illustrious past for future generations to discover and explore.

Napata, the first capital of Kush, occupies a central place in the history and heritage of ancient Africa. From its humble beginnings as a small settlement along the banks of the Nile to its rise as a powerful city-state and cultural center, Napata played a crucial role in shaping the destiny of the region and laying the foundations for the development of Kushite civilization. As we continue to study and explore the ruins of Napata, we gain a deeper appreciation for the richness and complexity of ancient African history and the enduring legacy of its remarkable achievements.

# Cultural Exchange and Artistic Flourishing of Kush: A Tapestry of Diversity and Creativity

The Kingdom of Kush, nestled along the banks of the Nile River in present-day Sudan, was not only a powerful political and military force but also a vibrant center of cultural exchange and artistic innovation. From its interactions with neighboring civilizations to its rich indigenous traditions, Kush fostered a diverse and dynamic cultural landscape that gave rise to a flourishing of artistic expression. In this chapter, we explore the cultural exchange and artistic achievements of Kush, tracing the influences and inspirations that shaped its unique cultural identity.

**Cultural Exchange with Egypt:**

One of the most significant influences on Kushite culture was its close relationship with Egypt, its northern neighbor. From the earliest interactions between the two civilizations, Kush absorbed many aspects of Egyptian culture, religion, and art, while also contributing its own unique traditions and innovations.

The Kushites adopted Egyptian gods and religious practices, such as the worship of Amun-Ra, the king of the gods, and the construction of monumental temples and pyramids dedicated to the gods. They also adopted hieroglyphic writing and artistic conventions, producing inscriptions, reliefs, and sculptures that mirrored Egyptian styles and themes.

At the same time, the Kushites infused Egyptian artistic forms with their own indigenous motifs and symbols, creating a distinctive hybrid style that reflected their cultural identity and heritage. For example, Kushite temples often featured depictions of indigenous flora and fauna, such as palm trees, lotus flowers, and lions, alongside traditional Egyptian iconography.

**Indigenous Traditions and Innovations:**

In addition to its interactions with Egypt, Kush also had a rich indigenous cultural heritage that shaped its artistic expression. The Kushites were skilled artisans, craftsmen, and architects who excelled in a variety of artistic mediums, including sculpture, pottery, metalwork, and textile weaving.

One of the most famous examples of Kushite artistry is the black granite statues of Kushite kings and queens, known as the "Black Pharaohs," which adorned the temples and palaces of Napata and Meroe. These statues, with their finely carved features and regal poses, exemplify the sophistication and elegance of Kushite artistic craftsmanship.

Kushite artists also produced exquisite pottery vessels, decorated with intricate geometric patterns, animal motifs, and symbolic designs. These vessels were used for a variety of purposes, including storage, cooking, and ritual ceremonies, and reflect the cultural significance of pottery in Kushite society.

**Religious and Spiritual Expression:**

Religion played a central role in Kushite culture, shaping every aspect of daily life, from politics and governance to art and architecture. The Kushites worshipped a pantheon of gods and goddesses, including Amun-Ra, the sun god; Anuket, the goddess of the Nile; and Apedemak, the lion-headed god of war.

Kushite temples, such as the Temple of Amun at Napata and the Temple of Apedemak at Meroe, were centers of religious activity and artistic expression, adorned with statues, reliefs, and inscriptions that celebrated the gods and goddesses of the Kushite pantheon. These temples served as places of worship, pilgrimage, and communal gathering, where Kushites came together to honor their gods and seek divine favor.

In addition to temples, Kushite culture also featured a rich tradition of funerary art and architecture, as evidenced by the royal pyramids and tombs of Napata and Meroe. These monumental structures, built of sandstone and granite, were adorned with hieroglyphic inscriptions, reliefs, and paintings that depicted scenes of the afterlife and the journey of the soul.

**Cultural Legacy and Influence:**

The cultural exchange and artistic flourishing of Kush left a lasting legacy that continues to resonate in the art, architecture, and culture of modern Sudan and beyond. The Kushite Kingdom may have faded into obscurity, but its achievements and contributions to the history of African civilization endure to this day.

As we continue to study and explore the cultural exchange and artistic achievements of Kush, we gain a deeper appreciation for the diversity, creativity, and resilience of its people. The story of Kush is a testament to the power of cultural exchange to inspire, innovate, and transform, creating a rich tapestry of human experience that transcends time and space.

# The Golden Age of the Kush Kingdom: A Flourishing Civilization Along the Banks of the Nile

The Golden Age of the Kush Kingdom represents a pinnacle of achievement and prosperity in the history of ancient African civilization. Spanning several centuries, this period witnessed unprecedented cultural, political, and economic development along the banks of the Nile River in present-day Sudan. From the reign of powerful monarchs to the construction of monumental architecture and the flourishing of artistic expression, the Kush Kingdom experienced a period of unparalleled growth and influence. In this comprehensive exploration, we delve into the key factors, achievements, and legacies of the Golden Age of the Kush Kingdom, unraveling the mysteries of this remarkable era in African history.

### Political Stability and Expansion:

The Golden Age of the Kush Kingdom was characterized by political stability and territorial expansion under the rule of powerful monarchs. Building upon the achievements of their predecessors, Kushite rulers consolidated their control over the Nile Valley, extending their influence northward into Egypt and southward into Nubia. The reigns of legendary kings such as Piye, Taharqa, and Aspelta marked a period of military conquests, diplomatic alliances, and administrative reforms that solidified Kushite dominance in northeastern Africa.

### Economic Prosperity and Trade:

Economic prosperity was a hallmark of the Golden Age of the Kush Kingdom, fueled by the kingdom's strategic location along major trade routes and abundant natural resources. The Nile River served as a lifeline for commerce, agriculture, and transportation, facilitating the exchange of goods, commodities, and luxury items between Kush and neighboring civilizations. Gold, ivory, incense, and exotic animals were among the valuable commodities traded by Kushite merchants, who established lucrative trade networks with Egypt, Nubia, Axum, and the Mediterranean world.

**Cultural Flourishing and Artistic Achievement:**

The Golden Age of the Kush Kingdom witnessed a flowering of cultural expression and artistic achievement, as evidenced by the monumental architecture, sculpture, and pottery produced during this period. The construction of temples, palaces, and pyramids reached new heights of grandeur and sophistication, reflecting the kingdom's religious piety, royal patronage, and technological innovation. The iconic Nubian pyramids of Meroe, with their distinctive design and decorative elements, stand as enduring symbols of Kushite artistic prowess and architectural ingenuity.

**Religious Revival and Spiritual Renewal:**

Religious revival and spiritual renewal were integral aspects of the Golden Age of the Kush Kingdom, as the ruling elite sought to reaffirm their divine authority and cosmic significance. The worship of indigenous deities such as Apedemak, Amun, and Isis flourished alongside Egyptian gods and goddesses, reflecting a syncretic religious tradition that combined elements of indigenous African and foreign influences. Temples, shrines, and cult centers dedicated to the gods and goddesses of Kush proliferated throughout the kingdom, serving as focal points of religious devotion and ritual practice.

**Intellectual Advancement and Cultural Exchange:**

The Golden Age of the Kush Kingdom was a period of intellectual advancement and cultural exchange, as scholars, scribes, and artisans thrived in an atmosphere of learning and creativity. The kingdom's cosmopolitan cities, such as Napata, Meroe, and Kerma, attracted scholars and craftsmen from diverse ethnic and cultural backgrounds, fostering a climate of intellectual curiosity and artistic innovation. The translation of texts, the exchange of ideas, and the patronage of the arts contributed to the enrichment of Kushite culture and the dissemination of knowledge throughout the region.

**Legacy of the Golden Age of the Kush Kingdom:**
The legacy of the Golden Age of the Kush Kingdom endures as a testament to the ingenuity, creativity, and resilience of ancient African civilization. The achievements and advancements of this remarkable era continue to inspire awe and admiration among scholars, artists, and enthusiasts of Kushite history and culture. As we unravel the mysteries of the Golden Age of the Kush Kingdom, we gain a deeper appreciation for the enduring legacy of this flourishing civilization and its enduring contributions to the cultural heritage of Africa and the world.

The Golden Age of the Kush Kingdom represents a period of unparalleled achievement and prosperity in the history of ancient African civilization. From political stability and territorial expansion to economic prosperity and cultural flourishing, the Kush Kingdom reached new heights of power and influence along the banks of the Nile River. The legacy of this remarkable era continues to inspire fascination and admiration among scholars and enthusiasts, shedding light on the enduring achievements and contributions of the Kushite civilization to the cultural heritage of Africa and the world.

# Exploring the Magnificence of the Temple Complexes of Kush: Architectural Marvels of Ancient Africa

The temple complexes of Kush, , stand as testaments to the architectural prowess, religious devotion, and cultural sophistication of the Kushite civilization. From the grandeur of Napatan temples to the elegance of Meroitic sanctuaries, these sacred sites served as centers of worship, pilgrimage, and cultural exchange, leaving behind a legacy that continues to inspire awe and admiration. In this comprehensive exploration, we delve into the temple complexes of Kush, unraveling their mysteries, unraveling their mysteries, and uncovering their significance in the annals of ancient African history.

**Napatan Temple Complexes:**

The Napatan period (c. 800–300 BCE) witnessed the construction of some of the earliest and most iconic temple complexes in Kush, as the Kushite kings sought to assert their religious authority and divine legitimacy. The most famous of these temples is the Temple of Amun at Jebel Barkal, located near the modern town of Karima.

The Temple of Amun at Jebel Barkal was built during the reign of King Taharqa, one of the most powerful and influential Kushite pharaohs. The temple complex consists of a main sanctuary, a processional way, and a sacred lake, surrounded by a massive enclosure wall adorned with reliefs, inscriptions, and statues of gods and pharaohs.

Another notable Napatan temple complex is the Temple of Amun at Naqa, located near the ancient city of Meroe. This temple complex features a monumental pylon entrance, a hypostyle hall, and a sanctuary, adorned with elaborate carvings, painted reliefs, and inscriptions honoring the gods and goddesses of the Kushite pantheon.

**Meroitic Temple Complexes:**

During the Meroitic period (c. 300 BCE–AD 350), the temple complexes of Kush underwent a transformation, as the Kushite rulers adopted new architectural styles and religious practices influenced by Egyptian, Greek, and Roman traditions. The most prominent Meroitic temple complex is the Temple of Amun at Musawwarat es-Sufra, located near the modern town of Shendi.

The Temple of Amun at Musawwarat es-Sufra is one of the largest and most well-preserved temple complexes in Kush, covering an area of over 45,000 square meters. The complex consists of a main temple dedicated to the god Amun, surrounded by smaller shrines, chapels, and courtyards, all adorned with intricate carvings, painted reliefs, and inscriptions.

Another notable Meroitic temple complex is the Temple of Apedemak at Naqa, dedicated to the lion-headed god of war and protection. This temple complex features a unique tripartite design, with three sanctuaries arranged in a row, each adorned with statues, reliefs, and inscriptions honoring Apedemak and other deities.


**Architectural Features and Decorations:**

The temple complexes of Kush are characterized by their distinctive architectural features and decorative elements, which reflect the unique blend of indigenous, Egyptian, and Greco-Roman influences. The temples are typically constructed of sandstone, granite, and limestone, with massive pylons, towering columns, and elaborately carved facades.

The exteriors of the temples are adorned with intricate carvings, painted reliefs, and hieroglyphic inscriptions that depict scenes from mythology, history, and religious rituals. The interiors of the temples are equally impressive, with hypostyle halls, offering chambers, and sanctuaries adorned with statues, altars, and ritual implements.

One of the most striking features of Kushite temple architecture is the use of colossal statues, known as colossi, which adorned the entrances to temples and lined the processional ways leading to the sacred precincts. These statues, carved from granite or sandstone, depict gods, pharaohs, and mythical creatures in majestic poses, symbolizing the power and authority of the divine.

**Religious Significance and Ritual Practices:**

The temple complexes of Kush served as centers of religious worship, pilgrimage, and ritual activity, where priests and devotees gathered to honor the gods and goddesses of the Kushite pantheon. The temples were the focal points of religious festivals, processions, and ceremonies, during which offerings, prayers, and sacrifices were made to ensure the favor of the gods and the prosperity of the kingdom.

The most important deity worshiped in the Kushite temples was Amun, the king of the gods, who was associated with the sun, fertility, and kingship. Other important deities worshiped in the temples included Apedemak, the lion-headed god of war; Anuket, the goddess of the Nile; and Osiris, the god of the afterlife.

The temple complexes of Kush stand as enduring symbols of the cultural, religious, and architectural achievements of the Kushite civilization. From the grandeur of Napatan temples to the elegance of Meroitic sanctuaries, these sacred sites reflect the ingenuity, creativity, and spiritual devotion of the Kushite people, who left behind a legacy that continues to inspire wonder and admiration to this day.

# Pyramids and Royal Tombs of Kush: Architectural Marvels and Cultural Significance

The pyramids and royal tombs of Kush, located along the banks of the Nile River in present-day Sudan, stand as enduring symbols of the power, wealth, and religious beliefs of the Kushite civilization. From the majestic pyramids of Napata to the elaborate burial chambers of Meroe, these monumental structures served as final resting places for Kushite kings and queens, as well as centers of religious worship and cultural significance. In this comprehensive exploration, we delve into the pyramids and royal tombs of Kush, unraveling their mysteries, uncovering their secrets, and uncovering their secrets, and shedding light on their enduring legacy in the annals of ancient African history.

**The Pyramids of Napata:**

The pyramids of Napata, located near the modern town of Karima, are among the earliest and most iconic pyramids in Kush. Built during the Napatan period (c. 800–300 BCE), these pyramids served as royal tombs for the Kushite kings and queens, who were believed to be divine rulers descended from the gods.

The most famous of the Napatan pyramids is the pyramid of King Taharqa, one of the most powerful and influential pharaohs of Kush. The Taharqa pyramid is the largest and most well-preserved pyramid in Napata, standing over 50 meters tall and featuring a limestone casing adorned with hieroglyphic inscriptions and reliefs depicting scenes from Taharqa's reign.

Other notable Napatan pyramids include the pyramids of King Piye, King Shabaka, and Queen Amanitore, each of which is distinguished by its unique architectural features, decorative elements, and religious symbolism. The pyramids of Napata served not only as royal tombs but also as symbols of the divine kingship of the Kushite rulers, who were believed to be intermediaries between the gods and the people.

**The Pyramids of Meroe:**

The pyramids of Meroe, located near the modern town of Begrawiya, are among the most striking and well-preserved pyramids in Kush. Built during the Meroitic period (c. 300 BCE–AD 350), these pyramids served as burial monuments for the Meroitic kings and queens, who continued the tradition of pyramid construction established by their Napatan predecessors.

The Meroitic pyramids are characterized by their distinctive architectural style, featuring steep, narrow angles, small chambers, and elaborate decorative elements. Unlike the smooth-sided pyramids of Egypt, the Meroitic pyramids have stepped, tiered exteriors, with each layer adorned with protruding pilasters, recessed panels, and cavetto cornices.

One of the most impressive features of the Meroitic pyramids is their decorative motifs, which include intricate carvings, painted reliefs, and hieroglyphic inscriptions that depict scenes from mythology, history, and religious rituals. These decorations served not only as adornments but also as expressions of the religious beliefs and cultural identity of the Meroitic people.

**Royal Tombs and Burial Practices:**

In addition to the pyramids, the royal tombs of Kush also include underground burial chambers, shaft graves, and funerary temples, which were used for the interment and commemoration of the deceased rulers and their families. The royal tombs are typically located beneath the pyramids, accessed via steep staircases or narrow passageways that lead to the burial chambers below.

The burial chambers of the royal tombs are often decorated with painted murals, inscriptions, and reliefs that depict scenes from the afterlife, including the journey of the soul, the judgment of the deceased, and the rituals of burial and resurrection. These decorations served as reminders of the religious beliefs and funerary practices of the Kushite people, who believed in the existence of an afterlife and the importance of proper burial rites.

The royal tombs also contain a variety of burial goods and offerings, including jewelry, pottery, weapons, and food, which were placed in the tombs to accompany the deceased on their journey to the afterlife. These funerary offerings were believed to provide the deceased with sustenance, protection, and comfort in the next world, ensuring their eternal happiness and well-being.

**Cultural Significance and Legacy:**

The pyramids and royal tombs of Kush are not only architectural marvels but also cultural symbols of the wealth, power, and religious beliefs of the Kushite civilization. From the grandeur of Napatan pyramids to the elegance of Meroitic burial chambers, these monumental structures reflect the ingenuity, creativity, and spiritual devotion of the Kushite people, who left behind a legacy that continues to inspire wonder and admiration to this day.

As we continue to study and explore the pyramids and royal tombs of Kush, we gain a deeper appreciation for the achievements and contributions of the Kushite civilization to the history and culture of ancient Africa. The story of the pyramids and royal tombs of Kush is a testament to the enduring legacy of one of the greatest civilizations of the ancient world, whose achievements continue to inspire awe and admiration in the modern age.

# Kushite Architecture and Engineering: Innovations, Marvels, and Legacy

The architecture and engineering of the Kingdom of Kush, located along the banks of the Nile River , stand as remarkable achievements of ancient African civilization. From the monumental temples and pyramids to the sophisticated irrigation systems and urban planning, Kushite architecture and engineering reflect the ingenuity, creativity, and technical prowess of its builders. In this comprehensive exploration, we delve into the innovations, marvels, and legacy of Kushite architecture and engineering, unraveling the secrets of their construction and shedding light on their enduring significance in the annals of human history.

**Urban Planning and Infrastructure:**

The urban centers of the Kingdom of Kush, such as Napata, Meroe, and Kerma, were meticulously planned and constructed, with well-defined street grids, organized neighborhoods, and centralized administrative complexes. The layout of these cities reflects the strategic positioning of important buildings, such as temples, palaces, and markets, as well as the efficient use of natural resources, such as water, sunlight, and wind.

One of the most impressive examples of Kushite urban planning is the city of Meroe, which served as the capital of the Meroitic Kingdom from the 3rd century BCE to the 4th century CE. The city features a grid-like street layout, with residential areas, industrial zones, and religious precincts arranged around a central core. The city also boasts a sophisticated water management system, with aqueducts, reservoirs, and canals that supplied water to the population and supported agricultural activities.

Another example of Kushite urban planning is the city of Kerma, which served as the capital of the Kingdom of Kerma during the Middle

Kingdom period (c. 2055–1650 BCE). The city is characterized by its defensive fortifications, including massive mud-brick walls and watchtowers, which protected the inhabitants from external threats and provided a sense of security and stability.

**Temple Architecture and Construction:**

The temple complexes of Kush are among the most impressive and enduring architectural achievements of the civilization, serving as centers of religious worship, political power, and cultural exchange. The temples were typically constructed of sandstone, granite, and limestone, with massive pylons, towering columns, and elaborately carved facades that reflected the grandeur and majesty of the gods they honored.

One of the most famous Kushite temples is the Temple of Amun at Jebel Barkal, located near the modern town of Karima. Built during the Napatan period (c. 800–300 BCE), this temple complex consists of a main sanctuary, a processional way, and a sacred lake, surrounded by a massive enclosure wall adorned with reliefs, inscriptions, and statues of gods and pharaohs.

Another notable Kushite temple is the Temple of Amun at Musawwarat es-Sufra, located near the modern town of Shendi. Built during the Meroitic period (c. 300 BCE–AD 350), this temple complex features a main temple dedicated to the god Amun, surrounded by smaller shrines, chapels, and courtyards, all adorned with intricate carvings, painted reliefs, and inscriptions.

**Pyramids and Funerary Architecture:**

The pyramids of Kush are among the most iconic and enduring symbols of the civilization, serving as royal tombs for the Kushite kings and queens and as monuments to their divine kingship. The pyramids were typically constructed of sandstone or granite, with stepped, tiered exteriors, small chambers, and elaborate decorative elements.

One of the most famous Kushite pyramids is the Taharqa pyramid, located near the modern town of Karima. Built during the Napatan period (c. 800–300 BCE), this pyramid stands over 50 meters tall and features a limestone casing adorned with hieroglyphic inscriptions and reliefs depicting scenes from Taharqa's reign.

Another notable Kushite pyramid is the pyramid of Queen Amanitore, located near the modern town of Meroe. Built during the Meroitic period (c. 300 BCE–AD 350), this pyramid is distinguished by its steep, narrow angles, small chambers, and elaborate decorative motifs, including carvings, reliefs, and inscriptions.

**Engineering Achievements and Innovations:**

The Kushites were skilled engineers who made significant contributions to the fields of irrigation, agriculture, and water management. One of the most impressive engineering achievements of the Kushites is the construction of the Qanats, underground tunnels that were used to transport water from the Nile River to the fields and settlements of the kingdom.

The Qanats were typically constructed of limestone or sandstone, with sloping shafts and horizontal galleries that allowed water to flow by gravity from higher elevations to lower elevations. The Qanats were equipped with sluice gates, channels, and reservoirs that regulated the flow of water and ensured a constant supply for irrigation and domestic use.

Another engineering innovation of the Kushites is the construction of dams, weirs, and reservoirs that were used to control flooding, store water, and regulate the flow of rivers and streams. One of the most famous Kushite dams is the Toshka Dam, located near the modern town of Abu Simbel. Built during the Napatan period (c. 800–300 BCE), this dam was constructed of mud-brick and stone, with sluice gates and spillways that allowed water to be diverted and stored for agricultural purposes.

**Legacy and Influence:**

The architecture and engineering of the Kingdom of Kush left a lasting legacy that continues to influence and inspire people around the world. From the monumental temples and pyramids to the sophisticated irrigation systems and urban planning, Kushite architecture and engineering reflect the ingenuity, creativity, and technical prowess of its builders, whose achievements continue to be celebrated and admired to this day.

As we continue to study and explore the architecture and engineering of Kush, we gain a deeper appreciation for the achievements and contributions of this remarkable civilization to the history and culture of humanity. The legacy of Kushite architecture and engineering serves as a testament to the enduring spirit of innovation, perseverance, and creativity that transcends time and space, leaving an indelible mark on the world for generations to come.

# The Kushite Military: Conquest, Defense, and Legacy

The military prowess of the Kingdom of Kush, situated along the banks of the Nile River in present-day Sudan, played a crucial role in the rise and fall of the civilization. From its early conquests of neighboring tribes to its later conflicts with powerful empires such as Egypt and Rome, the Kushite military demonstrated skill, courage, and resilience in both offense and defense. In this comprehensive exploration, we delve into the strategies, tactics, and achievements of the Kushite military, unraveling its conquests, defenses, and enduring legacy in the annals of ancient African history.

**Early Military Campaigns and Expansion:**

The Kingdom of Kush emerged as a regional power during the Napatan period (c. 800–300 BCE), with its kings launching military campaigns to conquer and annex neighboring territories. The early Kushite rulers, such as Piye and Shabaka, expanded their dominion southward into Nubia and beyond, establishing their authority over vast swathes of territory along the Nile.

One of the most famous Kushite conquests was the capture of the city of Elephantine, located at the First Cataract of the Nile, which served as a strategic stronghold and gateway to Upper Egypt. The Kushite kings built fortresses and garrisons along the Nile, allowing them to control trade routes, levy taxes, and extract tribute from conquered peoples.

The Kushite military also conducted expeditions into the deserts and oases of the Eastern Desert, where they established trading outposts, mining settlements, and military fortifications. These expeditions were aimed at securing valuable resources such as gold, ivory, and exotic goods, which were essential for the wealth and prosperity of the kingdom.

**Defense against External Threats:**

Throughout its history, the Kingdom of Kush faced numerous external threats from rival kingdoms, empires, and nomadic tribes, which sought to conquer, plunder, or subjugate the wealthy and powerful civilization. One of the greatest threats to Kush came from Egypt, its northern neighbor, which viewed Kush as a rival and potential enemy.

The Kushite military successfully defended against several Egyptian invasions, repelling attacks and launching counteroffensives that pushed the Egyptian forces back across the border. One of the most famous Kushite victories over Egypt was the defeat of Pharaoh Psamtik II at the Battle of Dukki Gel, where the Kushite army inflicted heavy casualties on the Egyptian forces and forced them to retreat.

In addition to Egypt, the Kingdom of Kush also faced threats from the Assyrian Empire, the Persian Empire, and the Roman Empire, all of which sought to expand their territories and influence into Africa. The Kushite military, with its skilled generals, disciplined soldiers, and strategic fortifications, was able to withstand these external threats and maintain the independence and sovereignty of the kingdom.

**Military Organization and Tactics:**

The Kushite military was organized into a professional standing army, consisting of infantry, cavalry, archers, and charioteers, as well as auxiliary units recruited from conquered peoples and allied tribes. The army was divided into regiments, battalions, and companies, each led by a commander or general appointed by the king.

The Kushite army employed a variety of tactics and strategies in battle, including frontal assaults, flanking maneuvers, and ambushes, depending on the terrain, weather, and enemy forces. The Kushite soldiers were skilled in hand-to-hand combat, using spears, swords, shields, and bows to engage and defeat their adversaries.

One of the most effective weapons in the Kushite arsenal was the war chariot, a light, maneuverable vehicle drawn by horses and equipped with archers and spearmen. The chariots were used to harass enemy formations, disrupt supply lines, and provide reconnaissance, reconnaissance, and reconnaissance support for the infantry and cavalry.

**Legacy and Influence:**

The military conquests and defenses of the Kingdom of Kush left a lasting legacy that continues to influence and inspire people around the world. From its early victories over neighboring tribes to its later conflicts with powerful empires, the Kushite military demonstrated skill, courage, and resilience in both offense and defense, leaving behind a legacy of valor and honor.

As we continue to study and explore the military history of Kush, we gain a deeper appreciation for the achievements and contributions of this remarkable civilization to the history and culture of humanity. The legacy of the Kushite military serves as a testament to the enduring spirit of bravery, perseverance, and determination that transcends time and space, leaving an indelible mark on the world for generations to come.

# The Kushite Response to External Threats: Challenges, Strategies, and Resilience

The Kingdom of Kush, faced numerous external threats throughout its history, ranging from rival kingdoms and empires to nomadic tribes and foreign invaders. These external challenges tested the resilience, ingenuity, and military prowess of the Kushite civilization, shaping its political, social, and cultural development. In this comprehensive exploration, we delve into the challenges posed by external threats to Kush, the strategies employed to address them, and the enduring legacy of Kushite resilience in the face of adversity.

**Historical Context: External Threats to Kush**

Since its emergence as a regional power during the Napatan period (c. 800–300 BCE), the Kingdom of Kush faced a series of external threats from neighboring kingdoms, empires, and nomadic tribes. These threats stemmed from geopolitical rivalries, territorial disputes, and competition for valuable resources such as land, water, and trade routes.

One of the earliest and most persistent threats to Kush came from its northern neighbor, Egypt, which viewed Kush as a potential rival and sought to expand its territory southward into Nubia. The frequent conflicts between Kush and Egypt, known as the Kushite-Egyptian Wars, were characterized by shifting alliances, territorial disputes, and military confrontations along the Nile River.

In addition to Egypt, Kush also faced threats from other neighboring kingdoms and empires, including the Assyrian Empire, the Persian Empire, and the Roman Empire, all of which sought to extend their influence into Africa and control the lucrative trade routes that passed through Kushite territory. These external threats posed significant challenges to the security, stability, and sovereignty of the kingdom, forcing Kushite rulers to adopt a variety of strategies to defend against them.

### Challenges and Responses: Strategies for Defense

The Kushite response to external threats was multifaceted, encompassing diplomatic negotiations, military alliances, fortifications, and strategic retreats, depending on the nature and severity of the threat. One of the key challenges faced by Kush was the defense of its northern border against Egyptian incursions, which required the construction of defensive fortifications, such as garrisons, watchtowers, and fortresses, along the Nile River.

The Kushite rulers also sought to maintain friendly relations with neighboring kingdoms and empires, such as the Kingdom of Axum and the Kingdom of Meroe, through diplomatic exchanges, marriage alliances, and trade agreements. These alliances served to strengthen Kush's position in the region and deter potential aggressors from launching military campaigns against the kingdom.

In times of crisis, when faced with overwhelming odds or imminent danger, the Kushite rulers were not afraid to adopt a policy of strategic retreat, withdrawing their forces from vulnerable positions and regrouping in fortified strongholds and mountainous terrain. This strategy allowed Kush to preserve its military strength and resources, while waiting for an opportune moment to launch counteroffensives against the enemy.

### Military Innovation and Adaptation

The Kushite response to external threats also involved military innovation and adaptation, as the kingdom sought to improve its defenses, tactics, and technology to meet the challenges of warfare in a changing world. One of the most notable innovations of the Kushite military was the development of new weapons, such as the composite bow, which combined the power and range of a traditional bow with the flexibility and durability of composite materials.

Another important innovation was the use of war chariots, light, maneuverable vehicles drawn by horses and equipped with archers and spearmen. The chariots were used to harass enemy formations, disrupt supply lines, and provide reconnaissance support for the infantry and cavalry, giving Kushite armies a decisive advantage on the battlefield.

In addition to weapons and tactics, the Kushite military also made significant advances in military engineering, constructing fortresses, citadels, and defensive walls that were designed to withstand prolonged sieges and assaults. These fortified strongholds served as strategic bastions of Kushite power, projecting influence and control over key territories and trade routes in the region.

**Legacy and Enduring Impact**

The challenges posed by external threats shaped the political, social, and cultural development of the Kingdom of Kush, leaving behind a legacy of resilience, adaptability, and determination that continues to inspire admiration and respect to this day. Despite facing overwhelming odds and formidable adversaries, the Kushite civilization persevered, overcoming adversity through innovation, diplomacy, and military prowess.

As we continue to study and explore the challenges of external threats faced by Kush, we gain a deeper appreciation for the achievements and contributions of this remarkable civilization to the history and culture of humanity. The legacy of Kushite resilience serves as a testament to the enduring spirit of courage, perseverance, and unity that transcends time and space, leaving an indelible mark on the world for generations to come.

# The Assyrian Invasion of Kush: Causes, Consequences, and Legacy

The Assyrian invasion of Kush, which occurred during the 8th and 7th centuries BCE, marked a significant turning point in the history of the Kingdom of Kush, situated along the banks of the Nile River in present-day Sudan. The invasion, led by the mighty Assyrian Empire, brought about profound political, social, and cultural changes in Kushite society, reshaping its geopolitical landscape and altering its relations with neighboring kingdoms and empires. In this comprehensive exploration, we delve into the causes of the Assyrian invasion of Kush, the consequences for both civilizations, and the enduring legacy of this pivotal event in ancient African history.

**Historical Context: Assyrian Expansion and Kushite Prosperity**

The Kingdom of Kush emerged as a regional power during the Napatan period (c. 800–300 BCE), with its kings conquering and annexing neighboring territories, including parts of Upper Egypt. The Kushite rulers established their capital at Napata, near the Fourth Cataract of the Nile, and developed a sophisticated civilization characterized by monumental architecture, religious fervor, and extensive trade networks.

Meanwhile, the Assyrian Empire, located in the ancient Near East, was undergoing a period of expansion and conquest under the leadership of powerful rulers such as Tiglath-Pileser III, Sargon II, and Sennacherib. The Assyrians sought to extend their influence into the Levant, Anatolia, and Egypt, establishing a vast empire that spanned from the Persian Gulf to the Mediterranean Sea.

**Causes of the Invasion: Geopolitical Rivalry and Territorial Ambitions**

The primary cause of the Assyrian invasion of Kush was geopolitical rivalry and territorial ambitions. The Assyrians viewed Kush as a potential threat to their interests in the Levant and Egypt, as well as a source of valuable resources such as gold, ivory, and slaves. Moreover, the Kushite kings had established diplomatic and trade relations with other regional powers, including the Kingdom of Israel and the Kingdom of Judah, which further heightened Assyrian suspicions and concerns.

Another factor that contributed to the Assyrian invasion of Kush was the desire to control trade routes and commercial centers in the Eastern Desert, which connected the Nile Valley to the Red Sea and beyond. The Assyrians saw Kush as a strategic obstacle to their ambitions of dominating the lucrative trade networks that passed through the region, prompting them to launch military campaigns to assert their authority and expand their influence.

**Consequences of the Invasion: Destruction, Displacement, and Cultural Exchange**

The Assyrian invasion of Kush had far-reaching consequences for both civilizations, reshaping the political, social, and economic landscape of the region. The Assyrians waged a brutal campaign of conquest and subjugation, destroying cities, plundering temples, and enslaving the population. Many Kushite cities, including Napata and Meroe, were sacked and looted, their treasures carried off to Assyria as spoils of war.

Thousands of Kushite refugees fled to neighboring kingdoms and empires, seeking sanctuary and protection from the Assyrian onslaught. Some migrated southward into Nubia, where they established new settlements and kingdoms, while others sought refuge in Egypt, Axum, and other regions of Africa and the Near East. The Assyrian invasion thus led to the displacement and dispersal of the Kushite population, contributing to the fragmentation of Kushite society and culture.

Despite the destruction and devastation wrought by the Assyrian invasion, it also had unintended consequences that contributed to the cultural exchange and interaction between the Assyrians and the Kushites. The Assyrians adopted elements of Kushite art, architecture, and religion, incorporating them into their own culture and identity. Likewise, the Kushites assimilated aspects of Assyrian culture, such as language, writing, and technology, into their own society, creating a synthesis of traditions and influences that enriched both civilizations.

**Legacy of the Invasion: Resilience, Adaptation, and Survival**

The legacy of the Assyrian invasion of Kush is one of resilience, adaptation, and survival. Despite the devastation and displacement caused by the invasion, the Kushite civilization endured, rebuilding and revitalizing itself in the aftermath of the conflict. The Kushite kings, such as Piye and Taharqa, rallied their forces, regrouped their allies, and launched counteroffensives against the Assyrians, reclaiming lost territories and asserting their independence.

Moreover, the Assyrian invasion of Kush served as a catalyst for cultural and political renewal within the Kushite kingdom. The Kushites adopted new military tactics, technologies, and strategies learned from their Assyrian adversaries, incorporating them into their own military repertoire and enhancing their capabilities on the battlefield. The Kushites also strengthened their alliances with neighboring kingdoms and empires, forging new diplomatic and trade relations that helped to consolidate their power and influence in the region.

The Assyrian invasion of Kush was a pivotal event in the history of ancient Africa, reshaping the political, social, and cultural landscape of the region. While the invasion brought destruction, displacement, and devastation to the Kushite civilization, it also sparked resilience, adaptation, and survival, as the Kushites rose to the challenge and emerged stronger and more united than ever before. The legacy of the Assyrian invasion of Kush serves as a testament to the enduring spirit of resilience, determination, and endurance that transcends time and space, leaving an indelible mark on the history and culture of humanity.

# The Decline of Kushite Power: Causes, Dynamics, and Legacy

The decline of Kushite power, once a formidable force in the ancient world, marks a significant chapter in the history of the Kingdom of Kush, situated along the Nile River in present-day Sudan. From its zenith during the Napatan and Meroitic periods to its eventual decline and fragmentation, Kush experienced a series of internal and external challenges that contributed to its waning influence and eventual demise as a major political and cultural power in the region. In this comprehensive exploration, we delve into the causes, dynamics, and enduring legacy of the decline of Kushite power, shedding light on the complex factors that led to its downfall and the lessons we can glean from its historical trajectory.

# Causes of Decline: Internal Strife, External Pressures, and Economic Decline

The decline of Kushite power was precipitated by a combination of internal and external factors that undermined the stability, prosperity, and cohesion of the kingdom. Internally, Kush was plagued by dynastic rivalries, succession disputes, and political instability, as competing factions vied for control of the throne and the resources of the kingdom.

Externally, Kush faced mounting pressure from rival kingdoms and empires, including Egypt, Assyria, and Rome, which sought to extend their influence into Africa and control the lucrative trade routes that passed through Kushite territory. These external pressures strained Kush's military and diplomatic resources, diverting attention and resources away from domestic governance and economic development.

Economically, Kush experienced a decline in its agricultural productivity, trade networks, and industrial output, leading to a deterioration in the standard of living and quality of life for its inhabitants. The decline of the Nile River's annual flooding, coupled with deforestation and soil erosion, reduced agricultural yields and disrupted food supplies, exacerbating social tensions and economic inequalities within the kingdom.

**Dynamics of Decline: Fragmentation, Invasion, and Cultural Assimilation**

The decline of Kushite power was characterized by fragmentation, invasion, and cultural assimilation, as rival factions vied for control of the kingdom and external powers sought to exploit its weaknesses for their own gain. The Kushite kingdom split into multiple rival states, each vying for supremacy and independence, leading to a protracted period of civil strife and internal conflict.

Externally, Kush faced invasion and conquest by powerful empires such as the Assyrian, Persian, and Roman Empires, which sought to extend their influence into Africa and control the valuable resources and trade routes of the region. These invasions weakened Kush's military and economic power, hastening its decline and eventual collapse as a major political and cultural force in the region.

Culturally, Kush underwent a process of assimilation and acculturation, as it came into contact with neighboring kingdoms and empires that had different languages, religions, and customs. The Kushites adopted elements of foreign cultures, incorporating them into their own society and identity, while also preserving and transmitting their own cultural heritage to future generations.

**Legacy of Decline: Lessons Learned and Enduring Influence**

The decline of Kushite power, while a tragic chapter in the history of ancient Africa, offers valuable lessons and insights into the dynamics of political, social, and economic change. The decline of Kush was not simply the result of external pressures or internal strife, but a complex interplay of factors that shaped the trajectory of its history and legacy.

As we reflect on the decline of Kushite power, we gain a deeper appreciation for the resilience, ingenuity, and creativity of its people, who faced adversity with courage and determination. The legacy of Kushite power serves as a reminder of the fragility of human civilization and the importance of solidarity, cooperation, and mutual respect in overcoming the challenges of an ever-changing world.

The decline of Kushite power is a cautionary tale of the rise and fall of civilizations, reminding us of the importance of vigilance, adaptability, and unity in the face of adversity. While Kush may have faded from the annals of history, its legacy lives on in the cultural, artistic, and architectural achievements of ancient Africa, inspiring future generations to strive for greatness and pursue their dreams with passion and purpose.

# The Rise of Axum: From Regional Power to International Empire

The rise of Axum, an ancient civilization located in present-day Ethiopia and Eritrea, marked a pivotal period in the history of the Horn of Africa and the broader region. From its humble beginnings as a small kingdom to its transformation into a powerful empire, Axum played a significant role in shaping the political, economic, and cultural landscape of ancient Africa. In this comprehensive exploration, we delve into the factors that contributed to the rise of Axum, the key milestones of its ascent, and the enduring legacy of its achievements.

# Historical Background: Origins and Early Development

The origins of Axum can be traced back to the pre-Aksumite period (c. 4th century BCE), when small agricultural communities began to emerge in the northern highlands of Ethiopia. These communities engaged in subsistence farming, animal husbandry, and trade with neighboring tribes, laying the foundation for the future prosperity and expansion of Axumite civilization.

During the 1st century CE, Axum began to emerge as a regional power, thanks in part to its strategic location along major trade routes connecting the Red Sea coast to the interior of Africa and the Arabian Peninsula. The kingdom's access to valuable resources such as ivory, gold, and frankincense enabled it to establish lucrative trade networks with neighboring regions, including Egypt, Arabia, and the Mediterranean world.

**Key Factors in the Rise of Axum:**

1. **Strategic Location:** Axum's location at the crossroads of trade routes linking Africa, Asia, and Europe gave it a strategic advantage in controlling the flow of goods and commodities between these regions. The kingdom's access to the Red Sea and the port of Adulis facilitated maritime trade with Arabia, India, and the Roman Empire, enriching Axumite merchants and merchants.

2. **Economic Prosperity**: The wealth generated from trade allowed Axum to develop a prosperous economy based on agriculture, commerce, and industry. The kingdom's fertile lands, terraced hillsides, and sophisticated irrigation systems enabled it to produce surplus food and agricultural products, which were traded for luxury goods and manufactured items from abroad.

3. **Political Stability:** Axum's ability to maintain internal stability and cohesion was crucial to its rise as a regional power. The kingdom

was ruled by a succession of powerful monarchs, known as neguses, who centralized authority, established a system of governance, and promoted social cohesion and unity among the diverse ethnic groups within the kingdom.

4. **Military Strength:** Axum's military prowess played a significant role in its rise to prominence, allowing it to expand its territory, defend its borders, and assert its authority over rival kingdoms and tribes. The Axumite army, composed of infantry, cavalry, and archers, was well-trained, disciplined, and equipped with advanced weaponry such as spears, swords, and shields.

**Key Milestones in Axum's Ascent:**

1. **Conquest of Yemen:** One of the defining moments in Axum's rise to power was its conquest of the Kingdom of Himyar in southern Arabia during the 3rd century CE. The Axumite king Ezana, also known as Abreha, launched a military campaign to subdue the Himyarite king Dhu Nuwas and establish Axumite control over the lucrative trade routes and ports of the Arabian Peninsula.

2. **Conversion to Christianity**: Another milestone in Axum's ascent was its conversion to Christianity during the 4th century CE. King Ezana, inspired by the teachings of the Christian faith, embraced Christianity as the state religion and promoted its spread throughout the kingdom. This religious transformation had profound implications for Axumite society, culture, and identity, establishing Christianity as a defining characteristic of Axumite civilization.

3. **Architectural Achievements:** Axum's rise to power was accompanied by a flourishing of architectural and artistic achievements, as evidenced by the construction of monumental structures such as obelisks, stelae, and palaces. The most famous of these is the Great Stela of Axum, a towering monument erected by King Ezana to commemorate his victory over the Kingdom of Himyar and his conversion to Christianity.

4. **Maritime Expansion:** Axum's maritime expansion during the 4th and 5th centuries CE extended its influence across the Red Sea and into the Indian Ocean, establishing trade links with India, Sri Lanka, and the Byzantine Empire. Axumite merchants sailed the seas in search of exotic goods such as spices, textiles, and precious metals, enriching the kingdom and enhancing its prestige on the international stage.

**Legacy of Axum:**

The rise of Axum left a lasting legacy that continues to influence the political, cultural, and religious landscape of modern Ethiopia and Eritrea. The kingdom's conversion to Christianity laid the foundation for the development of Ethiopian Orthodox Christianity, which remains the dominant religion in the region to this day.

Axum's architectural and artistic achievements, including its monumental stelae and rock-cut churches, are celebrated as symbols of Ethiopia's ancient heritage and cultural identity. The Great Stela of Axum, in particular, stands as a testament to the kingdom's power, prosperity, and religious devotion, inspiring awe and admiration among visitors and scholars alike.

The rise of Axum represents a remarkable chapter in the history of ancient Africa, showcasing the achievements and contributions of a civilization that once stood at the crossroads of continents and cultures. From its humble beginnings as a small agricultural community to its transformation into a powerful empire, Axum's ascent to prominence serves as a testament to the ingenuity, resilience, and vision of its people, who left an indelible mark on the history and culture of the Horn of Africa and the world beyond.

# Kushite-Axumite Relations: A Complex Interplay of Politics, Trade, and Culture

The relationship between the Kingdom of Kush and the Kingdom of Axum, two ancient civilizations located in northeastern Africa, was characterized by a dynamic interplay of politics, trade, and culture. Situated along major trade routes connecting Africa, Arabia, and the Mediterranean world, Kush and Axum enjoyed periods of cooperation, rivalry, and cultural exchange that left a lasting imprint on the history and development of the region. In this comprehensive exploration, we delve into the complex dynamics of Kushite-Axumite relations, examining the factors that shaped their interactions, the key milestones of their engagement, and the enduring legacy of their relationship.

The Kingdom of Kush, controlled vital trade routes and valuable resources such as gold, ivory, and frankincense, establishing lucrative trade networks with neighboring kingdoms and empires.

The Kingdom of Axum, located in present-day Ethiopia and Eritrea, also rose to prominence during the same period, thanks to its strategic location along major trade routes connecting the Red Sea coast to the interior of Africa and the Arabian Peninsula. Axum prospered from trade with Arabia, India, and the Roman Empire, becoming a wealthy and powerful kingdom in its own right.

**Factors Shaping Kushite-Axumite Relations:**

1. **Trade and Commerce:** One of the primary factors driving Kushite-Axumite relations was trade and commerce. Both civilizations were major players in the transcontinental trade networks that connected Africa, Arabia, and the Mediterranean world, facilitating the exchange of goods, commodities, and ideas.

2. **Political Alliances and Rivalries:** Kush and Axum often formed alliances and engaged in diplomatic relations with each other, particularly in response to external threats from neighboring kingdoms and empires. However, they also competed for control of strategic territories, trade routes, and natural resources, leading to periods of rivalry and conflict.

3. **Cultural Exchange:** Kushite-Axumite relations were characterized by a rich exchange of culture, language, religion, and technology. The Kushites and Axumites shared linguistic and cultural similarities, as well as religious practices influenced by Judaism, Christianity, and indigenous beliefs.

4. **Military Cooperation:** At times, Kush and Axum cooperated militarily to defend their territories and interests against common enemies. This cooperation included joint military campaigns, alliances, and treaties aimed at maintaining stability and security in the region.

**Key Milestones in Kushite-Axumite Relations:**

1. **Diplomatic and Trade Relations:** Throughout their history, Kush and Axum maintained diplomatic and trade relations with each other, exchanging ambassadors, gifts, and commodities. The Kushite capital of Meroe served as a major trading hub for goods imported from Axum, including luxury items such as spices, textiles, and precious metals.

2. **Military Conflicts and Alliances:** Despite periods of cooperation, Kush and Axum also engaged in military conflicts and alliances, particularly over control of strategic territories and trade routes. One notable conflict occurred during the 3rd century CE when Axum invaded Kush and sacked the city of Meroe, weakening Kushite power in the region.

3. **Religious Influence:** The spread of Christianity in the region during the 4th century CE had a profound impact on Kushite-Axumite relations. Axumite missionaries, inspired by the teachings of Christianity, traveled to Kush to spread the gospel, converting many

Kushites to the new faith and establishing churches and monasteries throughout the kingdom.

4. **Economic Cooperation**: Kush and Axum collaborated economically through joint ventures, trade agreements, and infrastructure projects aimed at promoting commerce and development in the region. Axumite merchants traveled to Kush to trade goods such as textiles, pottery, and glassware, while Kushite traders exported gold, ivory, and exotic animals to Axum.

**Legacy of Kushite-Axumite Relations:**

The legacy of Kushite-Axumite relations is evident in the cultural, linguistic, and religious heritage of modern Ethiopia and Eritrea. The exchange of ideas, technologies, and beliefs between Kush and Axum enriched the cultural tapestry of the region, shaping its identity and identity.

Kushite-Axumite relations were characterized by a complex interplay of politics, trade, and culture that shaped the history and development of northeastern Africa. Despite periods of cooperation and conflict, Kush and Axum maintained a dynamic relationship that left an indelible mark on the region's cultural, economic, and political landscape. Their legacy continues to resonate in the modern-day countries of Ethiopia and Eritrea, where the influence of Kush and Axum is still felt in the language, religion, and traditions of the people.

# The End of Kushite Independence: Causes, Consequences, and Legacy

The end of Kushite independence marked a significant turning point in the history of the Kingdom of Kush, situated along the banks of the Nile River in present-day Sudan. From its emergence as a regional power during the Napatan and Meroitic periods to its eventual decline and annexation by external forces, Kush faced a series of internal and external challenges that contributed to the erosion of its sovereignty and independence. In this comprehensive exploration, we delve into the causes of the end of Kushite independence, the consequences for the kingdom and the broader region, and the enduring legacy of this pivotal event in ancient African history.

**The Sunset of Kushite Power:**

However, Kush began to decline in the face of internal strife, external pressures, and economic challenges. Rival factions vied for control of the throne, while neighboring kingdoms and empires sought to assert their dominance over Kushite territory. The decline of Kushite power paved the way for the end of its independence and the eventual annexation by external forces.

**Causes of the End of Kushite Independence:**

1. **External Invasions:** One of the primary causes of the end of Kushite independence was external invasions by powerful neighboring kingdoms and empires. Throughout its history, Kush faced incursions from the Assyrians, Persians, and Romans, who sought to extend their influence into Africa and control the valuable resources and trade routes of the region.

2. **Internal Dissent and Rebellion**: Kushite society was plagued by internal dissent, rebellion, and political instability, as rival factions vied for control of the throne and the resources of the kingdom. Dynastic

rivalries, succession disputes, and social unrest weakened Kushite authority and undermined its ability to govern effectively.

3. **Economic Decline:** Kush experienced a decline in its agricultural productivity, trade networks, and industrial output, leading to economic stagnation and decline. The decline of the Nile River's annual flooding, coupled with deforestation and soil erosion, reduced agricultural yields and disrupted food supplies, exacerbating social tensions and economic inequalities within the kingdom.

**Consequences of the End of Kushite Independence:**

1. **Annexation by External Powers:** The end of Kushite independence resulted in the annexation of Kushite territory by external powers such as the Roman Empire, which sought to exploit the kingdom's resources and strategic location for their own gain. Kushite cities, including Napata and Meroe, were sacked and looted, their treasures carried off to foreign lands as spoils of war.

2. **Displacement of Population:** The end of Kushite independence led to the displacement and dispersal of the Kushite population, as thousands of refugees fled to neighboring kingdoms and empires in search of sanctuary and protection from the invading forces. Some migrated southward into Nubia, while others sought refuge in Egypt, Axum, and other regions of Africa and the Near East.

3. **Cultural Assimilation:** The annexation of Kushite territory by external powers resulted in cultural assimilation and acculturation, as Kushite society came into contact with foreign cultures, languages, and customs. The Kushites adopted elements of Roman, Greek, and Egyptian culture, incorporating them into their own society and identity, while also preserving and transmitting their own cultural heritage to future generations.

**Legacy of the End of Kushite Independence:**

The legacy of the end of Kushite independence is one of resilience, adaptation, and survival. Despite the devastation and displacement caused by external invasions and annexation, the Kushite civilization endured, rebuilding and revitalizing itself in the aftermath of the conflict. The Kushites continued to resist foreign domination and assert their independence, albeit in a diminished capacity, while preserving their cultural identity and heritage for future generations.

The end of Kushite independence marked the end of an era in the history of ancient Africa, signaling the decline and fragmentation of a once-powerful civilization that had dominated the region for centuries. While Kush may have fallen to external forces and lost its sovereignty, its legacy lives on in the cultural, artistic, and architectural achievements of ancient Africa, inspiring future generations to strive for greatness and pursue their dreams with passion and purpose.

# The Legacy of Kushite Rule in Egypt: Influence, Contributions, and Enduring Impact

The legacy of Kushite rule in Egypt, also known as the Twenty-fifth Dynasty or the Nubian Dynasty, represents a significant chapter in the history of ancient Egypt and the broader region of northeastern Africa. From their ascent to power during the Third Intermediate Period to their eventual decline and expulsion by the Assyrians, the Kushite pharaohs left a lasting imprint on Egyptian culture, religion, and politics. In this comprehensive exploration, we delve into the legacy of Kushite rule in Egypt, examining their influence, contributions, and enduring impact on the land of the pharaohs.

### The Kushite Conquest of Egypt

The Kushite conquest of Egypt occurred during the Third Intermediate Period (c. 1069–664 BCE), a time of political fragmentation and instability in ancient Egypt. The kingdom of Kush, located to the south of Egypt in present-day Sudan, had long-standing cultural and trade ties with its northern neighbor. However, it was not until the reign of King Piye (Piankhi) in the 8th century BCE that Kushite forces launched a successful military campaign to conquer Egypt and reunify the country under Kushite rule.

### Key Factors in Kushite Rule:

1. **Military Conquest:** The Kushite pharaohs, led by King Piye and his successors, employed military force to conquer and unify Egypt under their rule. The Kushite army, composed of infantry, chariots, and archers, overwhelmed the fragmented Egyptian states and established control over the entire Nile Valley, from the Delta to the southern frontier.

2. **Religious Legitimacy:** The Kushite pharaohs portrayed themselves as legitimate rulers of Egypt by invoking traditional Egyptian

religious and political symbolism. They adopted the titles, regalia, and religious rituals of the pharaohs of ancient Egypt, presenting themselves as heirs to the throne and defenders of the Egyptian gods and temples.

3. **Cultural Exchange**: Kushite rule brought about a period of cultural exchange and syncretism between Egypt and Kush. The Kushite pharaohs promoted the worship of Egyptian gods and goddesses alongside traditional Kushite deities, fostering a sense of religious pluralism and tolerance in Egyptian society.

4. **Architectural Projects**: The Kushite pharaohs undertook ambitious architectural projects to restore and embellish the temples and monuments of ancient Egypt. They commissioned the construction of new temples, shrines, and statues dedicated to the Egyptian gods, leaving behind a legacy of monumental architecture that still stands today.

**Contributions of Kushite Rule**:

1. **Religious Revival**: Kushite rule sparked a religious revival in Egypt, as the pharaohs sought to reinvigorate the worship of the traditional Egyptian gods and goddesses. They restored and renovated temples, conducted religious festivals, and patronized the priesthood, reviving the ancient religious traditions of Egypt.

2. **Political Unity:** Kushite rule brought about a period of political unity and stability in Egypt, as the country was reunited under a single ruler for the first time in centuries. The Kushite pharaohs established a centralized government, administered justice, and maintained order throughout the kingdom, ensuring peace and prosperity for their subjects.

3. **Cultural Renaissance**: Kushite rule ushered in a cultural renaissance in Egypt, characterized by a resurgence of artistic and intellectual activity. The Kushite pharaohs patronized artists, craftsmen, and scholars, fostering a climate of creativity and innovation that produced some of the finest works of art and literature in Egyptian history.

**Enduring Impact of Kushite Rule:**

1. **Religious Syncretism:** The legacy of Kushite rule in Egypt is evident in the religious syncretism that developed during this period, as Egyptian and Kushite religious beliefs and practices merged and evolved. The Kushite pharaohs introduced new gods and goddesses into the Egyptian pantheon, such as Amun-Ra, the principal deity of the Kushite dynasty, who became one of the most widely worshipped gods in Egypt.

2. **Architectural Heritage:** The architectural legacy of Kushite rule in Egypt is visible in the temples, pyramids, and monuments built or restored by the Kushite pharaohs. Their patronage of the arts and architecture enriched the cultural landscape of Egypt, leaving behind a legacy of monumental structures that continue to awe and inspire visitors from around the world.

3. **Cultural Exchange**: The period of Kushite rule facilitated cultural exchange and interaction between Egypt and Kush, fostering mutual respect and understanding between the two civilizations. Egyptian and Kushite artists, craftsmen, and scholars exchanged ideas, techniques, and materials, enriching the cultural heritage of both kingdoms.

The legacy of Kushite rule in Egypt is a testament to the enduring influence of Kushite civilization on the land of the pharaohs. Through their military conquests, religious revival, and cultural patronage, the Kushite pharaohs left an indelible mark on Egyptian history, shaping its religious, political, and artistic traditions for centuries to come. Their legacy continues to inspire fascination and admiration among scholars and enthusiasts of ancient Egypt, highlighting the dynamic interplay of cultures and civilizations in the ancient world.

# Meroe: The Last Capital of Kush - A Hub of Power, Culture, and Legacy

Meroe stands as a testament to the enduring legacy of the Kingdom of Kush, an ancient civilization that flourished as the last capital of Kush, Meroe played a pivotal role in shaping the political, economic, and cultural landscape of ancient Africa. From its strategic location as a hub of trade and commerce to its rich architectural heritage and religious significance, Meroe remains a source of fascination and intrigue for scholars and enthusiasts alike. In this comprehensive exploration, we delve into the history, significance, and enduring legacy of Meroe, the last capital of Kush.

### Rise of Meroe as the Capital of Kush

Meroe emerged as the capital of Kush during the Meroitic period (c. 300 BCE – 350 CE), succeeding earlier capitals such as Napata and Kerma. The relocation of the capital to Meroe marked a shift in Kushite political and cultural dynamics, as the kingdom expanded its influence and power southward along the Nile Valley.

### Key Factors in the Rise of Meroe:

1. **Strategic Location:** Situated at the confluence of the Blue Nile and Atbara Rivers, Meroe occupied a strategic position along major trade routes linking Egypt, Nubia, and the Red Sea coast. Its location facilitated trade and commerce with neighboring regions, enabling Meroe to prosper as a center of economic activity and exchange.

2. **Natural Resources:** Meroe's proximity to fertile agricultural lands and valuable natural resources, such as gold, iron, and ebony, contributed to its economic prosperity and political significance. The kingdom of Kush derived wealth and power from the exploitation of these resources, which fueled its expansion and development.

3. **Cultural and Religious Center:** Meroe served as a cultural and religious center of the Kushite civilization, boasting an impressive array

of temples, palaces, and royal tombs dedicated to the worship of Egyptian and indigenous deities. The city's religious significance attracted pilgrims, scholars, and artisans from across the region, fostering a climate of intellectual and artistic exchange.

4. **Architectural Legacy:** Meroe's architectural legacy is characterized by its distinctive style of pyramids, known as Nubian pyramids, which differ in design from their Egyptian counterparts. The Meroitic pyramids feature steep, narrow profiles, with small chapel-like structures attached to their eastern faces. These pyramids served as royal tombs for the Kushite monarchs, reflecting the kingdom's rich funerary traditions and religious beliefs.

**Significance of Meroe as the Capital of Kush:**

1. **Political Power:** As the capital of Kush, Meroe served as the seat of royal authority and government, housing the royal palace, administrative offices, and elite residences of the ruling class. The city was a symbol of Kushite sovereignty and independence, asserting the kingdom's status as a major political and military power in the region.

2. **Economic Prosperity**: Meroe's position as a center of trade and commerce contributed to its economic prosperity and wealth. The city served as a hub for the exchange of goods, commodities, and luxury items, including gold, ivory, incense, and exotic animals, which were traded with neighboring kingdoms and empires.

3. **Cultural Exchange:** Meroe's cosmopolitan atmosphere fostered cultural exchange and interaction between diverse ethnic and religious groups. The city was home to a multicultural population of Kushites, Egyptians, Greeks, Romans, and indigenous peoples, who coexisted and intermingled in a spirit of tolerance and mutual respect.

**Enduring Legacy of Meroe**:

1. **Architectural Marvels**: The legacy of Meroe lives on in its impressive architectural remains, including the iconic Nubian pyramids that dot the landscape surrounding the city. These pyramids, along with the ruins of temples, palaces, and fortifications, stand as a testament to the ingenuity and craftsmanship of the Kushite builders and artisans.

2. **Cultural Heritage**: Meroe's cultural heritage continues to inspire fascination and admiration among scholars and enthusiasts of ancient Africa. The city's rich artistic traditions, religious practices, and linguistic heritage have left an indelible mark on the cultural landscape of Sudan and the broader region, influencing subsequent civilizations and societies.

3. **Symbol of African Civilization**: Meroe symbolizes the achievements and contributions of ancient African civilization to the world. As the last capital of Kush, it represents the culmination of centuries of cultural, political, and economic development in the Nile Valley, showcasing the resilience, creativity, and sophistication of the peoples of ancient Africa.

Meroe, the last capital of Kush, stands as a beacon of power, culture, and legacy in the annals of ancient African history. From its strategic location as a center of trade and commerce to its rich architectural heritage and religious significance, Meroe embodies the spirit of Kushite civilization and its enduring contributions to the world. As we continue to unravel the mysteries of Meroe and explore its significance, we gain a deeper appreciation for the diversity and richness of Africa's ancient past, and the enduring legacy of its remarkable achievements.

# The Kushite Influence on African Culture: A Legacy of Power, Religion, and Artistic Expression

The Kingdom of Kush, an ancient civilization that thrived along the banks of the Nile exerted a profound influence on the cultural landscape of Africa. From its strategic position as a hub of trade and commerce to its rich religious traditions and artistic achievements, Kushite culture left an indelible mark on the peoples and societies of northeastern Africa and beyond. In this comprehensive exploration, we delve into the diverse aspects of Kushite influence on African culture, tracing its impact on religion, language, art, architecture, and societal norms.

**Key Aspects of Kushite Influence on African Culture:**

1. **Religious Syncretism:** Kushite religion was characterized by a blend of indigenous African beliefs and practices with influences from Egyptian, Greek, and Roman religious traditions. The Kushites worshipped a pantheon of gods and goddesses, including Amun, Isis, Osiris, and Apedemak, alongside indigenous deities such as Apedemak, the lion-headed god of war and protection. This syncretism contributed to the rich tapestry of religious diversity in ancient Africa and influenced subsequent religious movements in the region.

2. **Linguistic Legacy:** The Kushite civilization made significant contributions to the linguistic diversity of Africa through the development and dissemination of the Meroitic script, an indigenous writing system used for administrative, religious, and literary purposes. The Meroitic script, which was derived from Egyptian hieroglyphs but evolved into a distinct writing system, is one of the few indigenous African scripts to have been deciphered by modern scholars, shedding light on Kushite language and culture.

3. **Artistic Expression**: Kushite art and architecture were characterized by their distinctive style and iconography, which reflected the kingdom's cultural heritage and religious beliefs. The Kushites were renowned for their mastery of stone carving, metalworking, and pottery, producing exquisite sculptures, reliefs, and artifacts that adorned temples, palaces, and tombs throughout the kingdom. The iconic Nubian pyramids of Meroe, with their steep, narrow profiles and decorative elements, are among the most enduring symbols of Kushite artistic achievement.

4. **Architectural Marvels:** The Kushites were prolific builders, constructing impressive monuments, temples, and fortifications that reflected their political power and religious piety. The city of Meroe, the capital of Kush, was home to a wealth of architectural treasures, including the royal palaces, temples dedicated to Egyptian and indigenous deities, and the sprawling necropolis of pyramids and tombs that housed the remains of Kushite monarchs and nobles. These architectural marvels continue to inspire awe and admiration among visitors to Sudan, serving as a testament to the ingenuity and creativity of the Kushite builders and craftsmen.

5. **Societal Norms and Customs:** Kushite society was characterized by its social hierarchy, gender roles, and cultural traditions, which influenced the daily lives of its inhabitants. The Kushites practiced matrilineal inheritance, with descent and inheritance passing through the female line, and women held positions of authority and influence in both the royal court and the priesthood. The Kushites also valued education, literacy, and artistic expression, fostering a climate of intellectual and cultural flourishing that contributed to the kingdom's prosperity and stability.

**Legacy of Kushite Influence on African Culture:**

The legacy of Kushite influence on African culture is evident in the enduring impact of its religious, linguistic, artistic, and architectural traditions on the peoples and societies of northeastern Africa and beyond. The syncretic religious beliefs and practices of the Kushites continue to resonate in the religious diversity of modern Africa, while the Meroitic script serves as a reminder of Africa's rich linguistic heritage. The artistic achievements of the Kushites, manifested in their sculptures, reliefs, and monuments, inspire admiration and appreciation among scholars and enthusiasts of ancient African art. The architectural legacy of Kushite civilization, embodied in the majestic pyramids and temples of Meroe, stands as a testament to the kingdom's cultural and political achievements, serving as a source of pride and identity for the people of Sudan and the broader African continent.

The Kushite civilization exerted a profound and enduring influence on the cultural landscape of Africa, shaping religious beliefs, linguistic traditions, artistic expression, and architectural achievements for centuries to come. From its political power and economic prosperity to its rich religious and cultural heritage, Kushite culture continues to inspire fascination and admiration among scholars, artists, and enthusiasts of ancient Africa. As we continue to unravel the mysteries of Kushite civilization and explore its legacy, we gain a deeper appreciation for the diversity, complexity, and richness of Africa's ancient past, and the enduring contributions of its remarkable civilizations.

# Kings, Queens, and Gods of the Kush Kingdom: A Royal Pantheon of Power, Influence, and Devotion

The Kingdom of Kush,boasted a rich and vibrant royal pantheon comprised of kings, queens, and gods who wielded power, influence, and divine authority. From the legendary rulers of the Napatan and Meroitic dynasties to the deities worshipped in temples and shrines throughout the kingdom, the royal pantheon of Kush reflects the complex interplay of politics, religion, and culture in ancient Africa. In this comprehensive exploration, we delve into the lives, legends, and legacies of the kings, queens, and gods of the Kush kingdom, unraveling the mysteries of their reigns and the enduring impact they left on the history and culture of northeastern Africa.

The transition from the Napatan period to the Meroitic period marked a shift in Kushite political and cultural dynamics, as the capital of the kingdom was relocated to Meroe. The Meroitic kings and queens continued the legacy of their Napatan predecessors, expanding the kingdom's influence and power through military conquests, diplomatic alliances, and economic prosperity.

**Kings of Kush: The Pharaohs of the Nile**

The kings of Kush, also known as the pharaohs of the Nile, were revered as divine rulers endowed with divine authority and cosmic power. They traced their lineage back to the gods and goddesses of ancient Egypt, claiming descent from divine ancestors such as Amun, Ra, and Osiris. The pharaohs of Kush ruled over a vast and diverse kingdom, commanding the loyalty and allegiance of their subjects through military might, religious piety, and administrative efficiency.

**Some of the most renowned kings of Kush include:**

1. **Piye (Piankhi):** Known as the founder of the Twenty-fifth Dynasty of Egypt, Piye was a powerful ruler who successfully united Egypt and Kush under his rule. His conquest of Egypt marked the beginning of Kushite dominance over the Nile Valley, ushering in a period of political unity and cultural exchange between the two kingdoms.

2. **Taharqa:** Taharqa was one of the most illustrious pharaohs of Kush, ruling over a vast empire that encompassed Egypt, Nubia, and parts of the Levant. He was a patron of the arts and architecture, commissioning the construction of temples, palaces, and monuments throughout his kingdom.

3. **Aspelta:** Aspelta was a Meroitic king who ruled during a time of political and economic prosperity in Kush. He expanded the kingdom's borders, promoted trade and commerce, and fostered a climate of cultural exchange and artistic flourishing.

### Queens of Kush: The Divine Consorts and Rulers

The queens of Kush played a pivotal role in the political, religious, and cultural life of the kingdom, serving as divine consorts, advisors, and regents to the kings. They wielded considerable influence and authority within the royal court, often exerting their power behind the scenes to shape the destiny of the kingdom.

**Some of the most notable queens of Kush include:**

1. **Amanirenas:** Amanirenas was a warrior queen who led the Kushite resistance against the Roman invasion of Egypt in the 1st century BCE. She rallied her troops and launched a series of successful military campaigns against the Roman legions, inflicting heavy casualties and securing the independence of Kush from Roman rule.

2. **Amanishakheto:** Amanishakheto was a Meroitic queen who ruled alongside her husband, King Teriteqas, during a time of political upheaval and external threats. She defended the kingdom against

invading forces and promoted the worship of indigenous Kushite deities, fostering a sense of national pride and unity among her subjects.

3. **Shanakdakheto**: Shanakdakheto was a queen regnant of Kush who ruled in her own right, wielding power and authority as a divine monarch. She commissioned the construction of temples and monuments dedicated to the gods and goddesses of Kush, enhancing the religious and cultural prestige of the kingdom.

### Gods of Kush: Divine Guardians and Protectors

The gods of Kush were revered as divine guardians and protectors of the kingdom, worshipped in temples, shrines, and sanctuaries throughout the land. They embodied the forces of nature, fertility, and cosmic order, presiding over the affairs of mortals and intervening in human affairs in times of need.

**Some of the most prominent gods of Kush include:**

1. Apedemak: Apedemak was the principal deity of the Kushite pantheon, worshipped as the god of war, protection, and fertility. He was depicted as a lion-headed warrior wielding a spear and shield, symbolizing strength, courage, and divine favor.

2. **Amun**: Amun was a widely worshipped god in Kush, revered as the king of the gods and the creator of the universe. He was associated with the sun, fertility, and kingship, embodying the divine power and authority of the pharaohs of Kush.

3. **Isis**: Isis was a popular goddess in Kushite religion, worshipped as the divine mother, protector, and healer. She was venerated as the patroness of kings, queens, and commoners alike, offering solace, guidance, and divine intervention to those in need.

### Legacy of Kings, Queens, and Gods of Kush

The legacy of the kings, queens, and gods of Kush endures as a testament to the power, influence, and divine authority of the Kushite civilization. Their reigns and religious beliefs shaped the destiny of the kingdom, influencing the course of history and leaving an indelible mark on the culture and identity of northeastern Africa.

The legacy of the kings of Kush is reflected in the monumental architecture, artistic achievements, and military conquests of the kingdom, while the queens of Kush are remembered for their wisdom, strength, and leadership in times of crisis. The gods of Kush continue to be venerated as divine protectors and guardians of the land, worshipped in temples and shrines as symbols of divine favor and cosmic order.

The kings, queens, and gods of Kush represent a royal pantheon of power, influence, and devotion that shaped the destiny of the kingdom and left a lasting legacy on the culture and identity of northeastern Africa. From the legendary pharaohs who ruled over a vast empire to the divine consorts who wielded power behind the throne, and the gods who watched over the kingdom as divine protectors, the royal pantheon of Kush continues to inspire awe and admiration among scholars, artists, and enthusiasts of ancient African civilization. As we unravel the mysteries of their reigns and religious beliefs, we gain a deeper appreciation for the complexity, diversity, and richness of Kushite culture, and the enduring legacy of its remarkable rulers and deities.

# Debates and Controversies in Kushite Studies: Unraveling the Mysteries of an Ancient Civilization

The study of Kushite civilization, an ancient kingdom that flourished along the banks of the Nile River in present-day Sudan, has been the subject of ongoing debates and controversies among scholars, archaeologists, and historians. From questions surrounding the origins and development of the Kushite civilization to debates over its political structure, cultural identity, and interactions with neighboring civilizations, the field of Kushite studies is rife with complexities and contradictions. In this comprehensive exploration, we delve into the key debates and controversies in Kushite studies, examining the competing theories, interpretations, and evidence that shape our understanding of this enigmatic civilization.

**Origins and Development of Kush**:

One of the most enduring debates in Kushite studies revolves around the origins and development of the civilization. While some scholars argue for an indigenous origin of Kush, tracing its roots back to the Neolithic period and the emergence of complex societies in the Nile Valley, others propose external influences and migrations from neighboring regions as key factors in the formation of the kingdom. The discovery of ancient settlements, burial sites, and artifacts has fueled speculation about the cultural and ethnic diversity of Kush and its connections to other civilizations in northeastern Africa.

**Political Structure and Governance:**

Another area of debate in Kushite studies concerns the political structure and governance of the kingdom. While early interpretations characterized Kush as a centralized monarchy ruled by divine kingship, recent scholarship has challenged this view, suggesting a more decentralized and fluid system of governance characterized by regional autonomy and tribal alliances. The role of the pharaohs, queens, and local rulers in the administration of the kingdom remains a topic of contention, with conflicting interpretations of their power, authority, and relationship to the broader political hierarchy.

**Cultural Identity and Ethnicity:**

The question of Kushite cultural identity and ethnicity has sparked considerable debate among scholars, with competing theories and interpretations based on linguistic, archaeological, and historical evidence. Some scholars argue for a homogenous Kushite identity defined by shared language, religion, and material culture, while others emphasize the cultural diversity and heterogeneity of the kingdom, highlighting the presence of multiple ethnic groups, languages, and traditions within its borders. The relationship between Kushite culture and that of neighboring civilizations, such as Egypt, Nubia, and Axum, further complicates the issue of cultural identity and ethnicity.

**Interactions with Neighboring Civilizations:**

The nature and extent of Kushite interactions with neighboring civilizations, particularly Egypt, Nubia, and Axum, have been the subject of intense debate and speculation among scholars. While some scholars emphasize the role of Kush as a powerful and influential empire that exerted control over vast territories and trade routes, others argue for a more nuanced understanding of Kushite diplomacy, military campaigns, and cultural exchange. The impact of external influences on Kushite art, architecture, religion, and language remains a topic of ongoing research and debate.

**Religious Beliefs and Practices:**

Religious beliefs and practices in Kushite civilization have also been a source of debate and controversy among scholars. The worship of indigenous deities such as Apedemak, Amun, and Isis, alongside Egyptian gods and goddesses, suggests a syncretic religious tradition that combined elements of indigenous African and Egyptian religion. However, the precise nature of Kushite religious beliefs, rituals, and cosmology remains poorly understood, with conflicting interpretations based on archaeological evidence, textual sources, and comparative studies of religious practices in neighboring civilizations.

**Archaeological Discoveries and Interpretations**:

Archaeological discoveries in Kushite sites such as Napata, Meroe, and Kerma have provided valuable insights into the material culture, social organization, and economic activities of the civilization. However, the interpretation of these discoveries has been the subject of debate and controversy, with differing opinions on the significance, chronology, and cultural context of archaeological finds. The preservation and conservation of Kushite sites, as well as the ethical considerations surrounding archaeological excavation and research, further complicate the study of Kushite civilization.

Debates and controversies in Kushite studies reflect the complexities and challenges of unraveling the mysteries of an ancient civilization that flourished in the heart of Africa for over a millennium. From questions about the origins and development of Kush to debates over its political structure, cultural identity, and interactions with neighboring civilizations, the study of Kushite civilization continues to be a dynamic and evolving field of inquiry. By critically engaging with competing theories, interpretations, and evidence, scholars strive to deepen our understanding of Kushite culture, society, and history, shedding light on the enduring legacy of this remarkable civilization in the annals of African history.